big ideas for
smallspaces

by David Lansing
and
JoAnne Liebeler

Sunset Books
Menlo Park, California

contents

small inspirations | 4

big ideas | 10

SUNSET BOOKS

VICE PRESIDENT, GENERAL MANAGER:
Richard A. Smeby
VICE PRESIDENT, EDITORIAL DIRECTOR:
Bob Doyle
PRODUCTION DIRECTOR: Lory Day
OPERATIONS DIRECTOR: Rosann Sutherland
MARKETING MANAGER: Linda Barker
ART DIRECTOR: Vasken Guiragossian
SPECIAL SALES: Brad Moses

9 8 7 6 5 4 3
First Printing June 2006
Copyright © 2006, Sunset Publishing Corporation,
Menlo Park, CA 94025

STAFF FOR THIS BOOK

SENIOR EDITOR: Ben Marks
ART DIRECTOR: Alice Rogers
PHOTO EDITOR/STYLIST: JoAnn Masaoka Van Atta
PRINCIPAL PHOTOGRAPHER: Jamie Hadley
ILLUSTRATOR: Eric Ipsen
COPY EDITOR: Phyllis Elving
PRODUCTION SPECIALIST: Linda M. Bouchard
ASSOCIATE EDITOR: Carrie Dodson Davis
PREPRESS COORDINATOR: Danielle Johnson
INDEXER: Jennifer Block Martin
PROOFREADER: Michelle Pollace

For additional copies of *Big Ideas for Small
Spaces* or any other Sunset book, visit us at
www.sunsetbooks.com or call 1-800-526-5111.

Cover photograph: Thomas J. Story
Styling: Emma Star Jensen
Cover design: Vasken Guiragossian

Big Ideas for Small Spaces is organized into three main sections. "Big Ideas" takes you on a tour of small homes, room by room. "Big Concepts" focuses on simple design principles that can be put to use almost anywhere. Finally, the "Small Wonders" section spotlights a selection of space-saving products that are available today, plus a handful of innovative prototypes that could be coming to a store near you tomorrow.

big concepts | 122
maxing your space

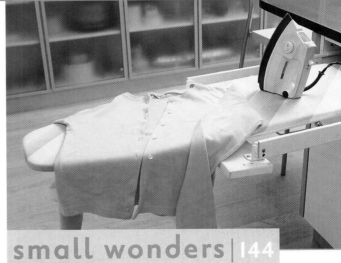

small wonders | 144
space-saving stuff

index | 156

Swiss Family Treehouse,
Disneyland

Have you ever thought about all of the places you've lived over the years? Focus in on the one or two rooms that were really, really special to you; odds are you're thinking of a small space, a room in which you felt snug, comfy, and, well, happy.

small inspirations

I've called 38 different places home. They've included a treehouse in Southern California, an Airstream trailer in Crete, and an elegant 350-year-old hacienda in Mexico. They had little in common architecturally, yet they all shared common denominators. Each was ingeniously designed, all made me feel incredibly secure (and, yes, happy), and every one of them has inspired remodels to the place I've called home for the past 19 years.

Now wait a minute, you say, you didn't *really* live in a treehouse, did you? For a summer or two when I was a kid, yes I did. You see, my father worked for Disneyland as a carpenter. One of my favorite projects was the Swiss Family Treehouse. I liked it so much that when I was 10, he built a miniature version of it in our backyard. Unlike the one he built for Uncle Walt, my treehouse had only one room, modeled after the Robinson boys' crow's nest. But my father incorporated a lot of elements from the Disney version, including his own ingeniously designed system of split bamboo to carry water from a garden hose to a shell basin so I could wash my face and brush my teeth. Little wonder that my friends and I spent as much time as we could in that treehouse, tricking it out with a trap door, a rope ladder, and an elaborate pulley system to open a section of the roof, allowing us to fall asleep under the stars.

As a 10-year-old, I thought my treehouse was the coolest place in the world. As an adult, that memory continues to delight and inspire. In fact, a number of details in my present house—from the bathroom's pedestal bowl fed by a high-arcing faux-bamboo spout faucet to the family room skylight that opens to reveal the moon and stars at night—are a direct result of that little backyard treehouse.

The treehouse was but the first of many small spaces that would inspire remodels years later. About 15 years after those treehouse summers, my wife and I wintered on the island of Crete in a rusting, enchanting, vintage Airstream trailer named Myrtle. Myrtle had an upper berth bed like those found on trains, but this one folded up and attached to the ceiling so that it was totally out of the way when not in use. Just as clever was the floor-to-ceiling chest of drawers

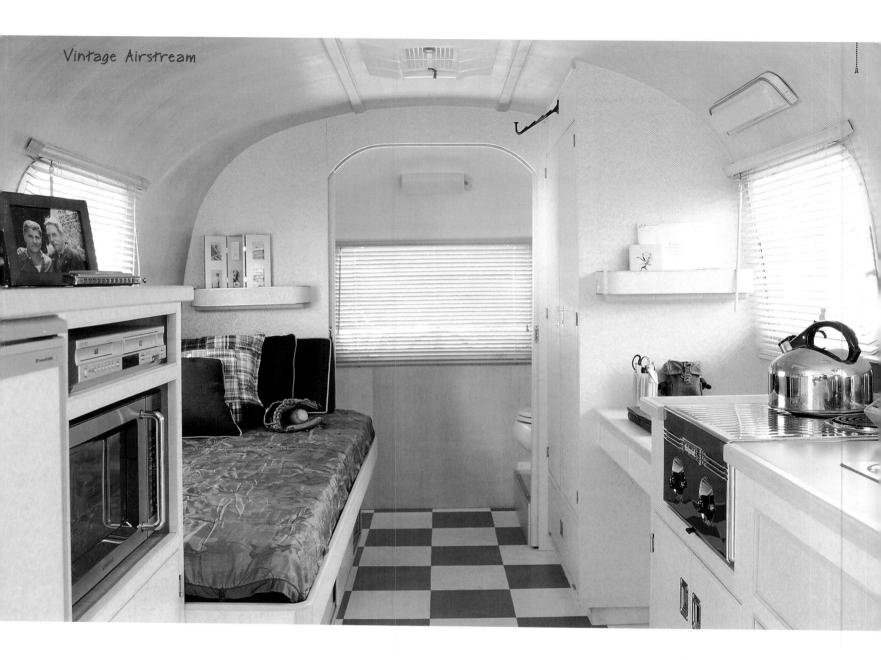

that provided critical storage space as well as serving as a room divider between the bathroom and the galley. You'd think that two people spending a winter in a 22-foot trailer would feel cramped, but Myrtle's thoughtful design nipped that potential problem in the bud. When we finally moved out of Myrtle and left Crete, we were as heartbroken as if we'd been forced to leave behind the family dog.

As it turned out, we never entirely left Myrtle behind. A couple of years ago, in the midst of yet another remodel to what was once a 700-square-foot beach bungalow but has grown into a home for a family of four, my wife was puzzling over how best to separate a bedroom from her home office without losing storage space. To complicate matters, we wanted the option of using the office as a guest room, but we didn't want a bed taking up precious floor space. We tried sketching out various solutions, but it wasn't until my wife exclaimed "Myrtle!" that the puzzle was solved: the wall between the bedroom and the office became a floor-to-ceiling storage system that included a Murphy bed behind a closet door. Who could have imagined that 25 years after that winter in Crete, Myrtle would solve a design riddle in a California home?

Our most recent remodel was inspired by a compact Colonial-era casa in San Miguel de Allende, where I lived several years ago for a few months while working on a book. No more than 15 feet wide, the house was a marvel of intricately woven small spaces. Two bedrooms on the bottom floor opened onto a courtyard via French doors, while upstairs the sight lines encompassed the dining room, the kitchen, and that same courtyard, which shel-

tered a small pond and a cluster of lemon trees that rustled in the breeze.

Needless to say, my wife and I found plenty of inspiration in that San Miguel casa. A windowless garden-facing wall at the back of our California house was replaced by French doors that now open onto a long, narrow patio lined with citrus trees and highlighted by a stone fountain. My home office in an 8-by-10-foot outbuilding in a corner of the yard has a bay window that nudges out into the garden. As I write this, hummingbirds flit around a flowering passion vine while painted lady butterflies dance on the breeze above the olive trees. Though my workspace is tiny, the bay window and a series of cleverly designed built-in cabinets make it feel several times its size. More important, it makes me feel calm and peaceful.

Continued >

Spanish-style courtyard

Of course, my wife and I are not the only ones who have been inspired by small spaces. Some of the world's best architects have long understood the effect small spaces can have on the people who live in them. That may explain why they design palatial mansions for their well-heeled clients but create more intimate spaces for themselves. One of my favorites actually reminds me very much of my old childhood treehouse. It's the Pacific Palisades, California, home of Charles and Ray Eames, the husband-and-wife design pioneers who, in 1949, built Case Study House #8. In a way, the Eames house is a lot like a boxy, two-story treehouse—albeit a 1,500-square-foot one—that sits on the ground. Built in a canyon in the middle of a eucalyptus grove, it gives you the feeling of being up at eye level with the treetops when you look out the windows.

Case Study House #8

The urge to create and inhabit such spaces is not limited to architects, who are trained to know better, or to people like me, whose remodels are governed largely by the realities of tight budgets. I remember visiting Julia Child at her condo in Montecito, California, some years ago. Here was one of the greatest American chefs, a woman whose famous Cambridge, Massachusetts, kitchen is enshrined in the Smithsonian, and yet her personal kitchen could not have been more modest. One wall was covered with a white pegboard filled with kitchen gadgets, eliminating the need for several drawers and cabinets. A small stove and oven stood right next to the sink. In fact, every appliance in the kitchen was no more than a step or two away.

"Someone told me it reminds them of a boat galley," she said.

I was thinking of how much it reminded me of the galley of that Airstream trailer in Crete.

big ideas
room by room

entry areas ⊚ living spaces ⊚ kitchens ⊚ dining rooms ⊚ bedrooms
⊚ bathrooms ⊚ home offices ⊚ transition spaces

A wall of glass allows light to flood into this entry area and stairway to a basement. A grid of translucent panes on an adjoining wall lets light into the kitchen behind it—a single pane has been left out of the grid to permit unimpeded visual flow between the two spaces.

entry areas

The function of an entry space is largely dictated by the natural environment. If you live in a climate with harsh or rainy winters, the entry room needs to be able to absorb the abuse of muddy sneakers, dripping umbrellas, and assorted rain gear—coats, hats, scarves, boots. Entry areas in more temperate climes, on the other hand, serve a different purpose. They become the architectural handshake welcoming family and friends, the first sign that says, "I'm home."

In either case, try to avoid space-eating walls that separate the entry area from the family or living room. A waist-high cabinet or shelving can serve the same function while doing double duty as a storage solution for much of that outdoor wear. On top of the cabinet, group family photos or collectibles—personal items that are expressions of your life.

A freestanding storage wall with cubicles can hold shoes and athletic gear. Or eliminate walls and cabinets completely, establishing a faux-entry room by using a low table or the back of the sofa as a "wall." A narrow entry table against the opposite wall can hold a small lamp, a plant, or fresh flowers. A piece of art in an entry area can become a focal point to establish the character of the house.

Sight lines are particularly important for a successful entry area. Door-facing walls create the feeling of cramped space, while open views that let the eye run diagonally through the house—from the family or living room and into the kitchen or dining room—seem to invite you in.

A simple wooden entrance area at the bottom of a flight of stairs is as straightforward and playful as a child's fort or treehouse.

This hardworking entry area has a built-in bench for sitting when putting on or removing shoes and boots, which can be stowed in baskets below. Above the bench, a handsome wooden rack handles coats and hats. There's even room for gardening tools.

Not only is this under-stairs storage nook a great solution to the problem of what to do with all those garden clogs, sneakers, and golf shoes, it's also a practical way to organize footwear; each family member gets his or her own shelf space for storage.

Less utilitarian than the mud-room shown on the facing page, this countrified entry space makes a strong design statement with its well-chosen artwork and throw rug, an eye-catching collection of walking sticks, and a small desk for paying bills—a task illuminated by an antique lamp.

great divide | this false wall opens to reveal a guest room

Some entry areas are open, offering uninterrupted views of a home's contents at a glance, others are designed to contain and separate. This one does both. Doors disguised as an attractive blond wood shelving unit (below) swing out and into a hidden guest room. The cabinets on the unit's left side present a neutral face to those entering the house, while the shelves on the right side are both decorative and functional.

Swivel wheels make the wall easy to move—by pushing the right side of
the unit into the guest room (above) or pulling the left side into the entry
room itself (inset), or both. Either move reveals a simple but comfortable
guest room, or perhaps a place for a family member to get away from it
all with a good book.

Picture windows keep this little room from feeling claustrophobic. They
admit lots of light, are hinged to let in fresh air, and visually bring the
outdoors inside. High ceilings also help; a library-style ladder on a track
makes it easy to reach the topmost shelves.

jojo's notebook

a sunny entrance

Color is the first "hello" visitors receive when entering this home. Its primary-yellow door is loud, proud, and a clear invitation to "C'mon in!" You can't always get away with such an audacious color in this small of a space, but it sure works here. The hue imparts a sunny playfulness, while the delightfully simple and childlike artwork just inside the door reinforces the effect.

Supporting players also contribute. The slate flooring lends elegance to the room, while the floor-to-ceiling compression-mounted shelf unit is long on simplicity, style, and practicality. Its open design and narrow profile prevent the unit from hogging too much real estate, and the tall, rectangular mirror catches light and creates the illusion of more space. Two free-standing walls differentiate the entry area from other rooms; one wall contains an unobtrusive guest closet. In short, I wouldn't change a thing.

JoJo

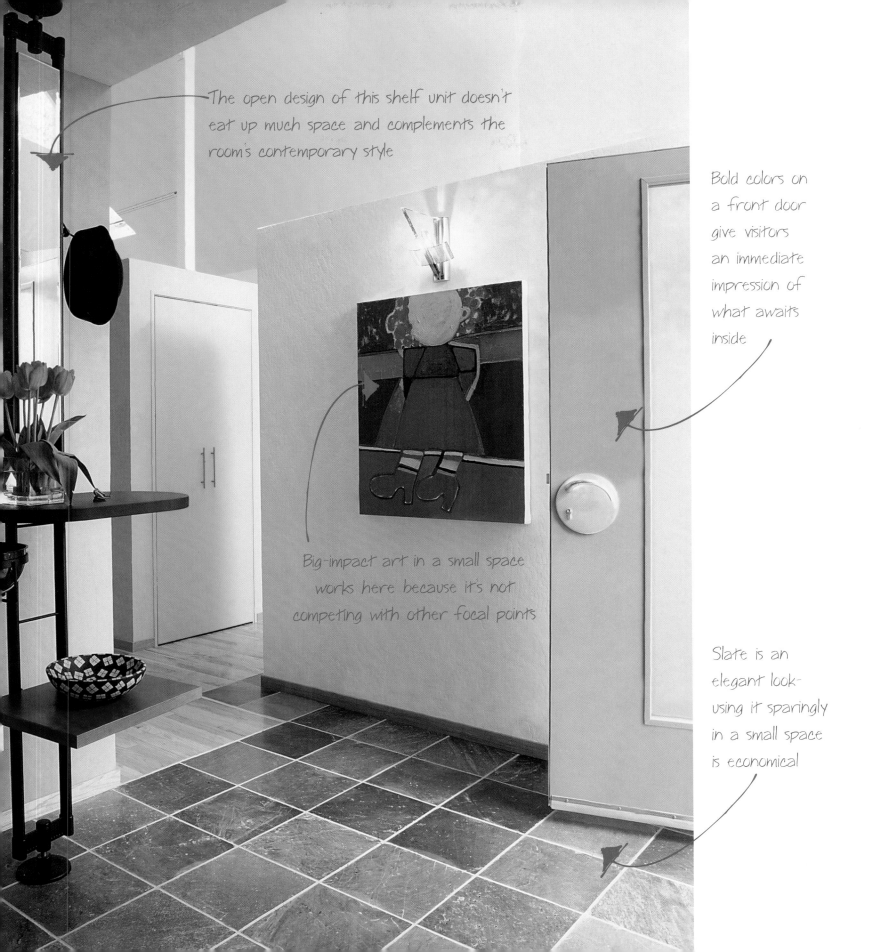

The open design of this shelf unit doesn't eat up much space and complements the room's contemporary style

Bold colors on a front door give visitors an immediate impression of what awaits inside

Big-impact art in a small space works here because it's not competing with other focal points

Slate is an elegant look- using it sparingly in a small space is economical

Back-to-back opium couches in this San Francisco apartment not only multitask as seating areas and guest beds but also creatively subdivide the living room. One side of the room functions as an entertainment area, while the other plays a more traditional role as a gathering space next to the kitchen and dining area.

living spaces

What's the difference between a living room and a family room? One gets used, the other doesn't. That's why, when faced with the choice of creating one or the other, many people choose a family room. This space where folks gravitate to entertain, watch a movie, play cards, take a nap, or read a book is easily the most multifunctional room in a house. That's why it needs special attention so it doesn't become your home's equivalent of the junk drawer.

The key to a successful small family room is to use only as much space as you really need for each of the room's functions and to keep traffic areas as open as possible. For instance, many people have a computer here, usually accompanied by a desk and additional equipment. Instead of giving up valuable floor space for an infrequently used full-size desk, consider carving an alcove out of one wall for a compact work area.

A window seat can be the perfect place to read a magazine or a book, allowing family members to have a cozy, separate space that's still within the boundaries of this gathering room. If you have small children, a bench seat can also be a good place to store toys.

If you do have a formal living room, hide away everything from your modem to your stereo equipment in a nearby closet or in a low-rise built-in cabinet. A flat-screen TV, hung on the wall, can eliminate the need for a special entertainment hutch or armoire.

Proportion and function are also important to keep in mind when choosing furniture for your living space.

Oversize chairs and couches look great in hotel lobbies, but they generally don't work well in smaller rooms. However, one properly proportioned couch, where everyone can sprawl to watch a movie, is better than multiple armchairs that take up more space and are visually fatiguing when crowded into a small space.

This alternate view of the apartment shown on the facing page reveals how a high breakfast counter, with wine storage built into one end, separates the kitchen from the living room.

The French doors opening off this living room help blur the line between inside and out. The sunny-colored wall accents the natural light streaming in, while the contrasting pale blue wall suggests an expansive sky or sea. A dark, solid color—like red—would have made the room feel less open.

This small room seems larger than it really is because of its floor-to-ceiling sliding glass door. In the center of the room, a neutral-colored couch seems to float above the dark floor; guests seated at the end of the couch can enjoy the window view as well as chat with people in the adjacent kitchen.

Leather-covered ottomans (above left) provide extra seating for guests but slip neatly under a small table when they need to be out of the way. The natural-grass runner in the living room above draws the eye down the narrow length of the room, accenting its deep dimensions.

Limiting the number of furniture pieces and choosing a flat-panel TV kept the circulation area in this low-ceilinged sitting room as open as possible. Hanging the TV on the wall gets one major element off the floor; placing the decorative planter on the raised hearth takes care of another.

Choosing just a few signature pieces of furniture (a classic Noguchi table, a Cherner armchair, and an Eames rocker), combined with the decision to build a low cabinet and display shelf along the far wall, left plenty of room for a hand drum in this tiny living room.

Open shelving makes room for books, knickknacks, and a window that lights up this small sitting area. Storage space below the window is used for pillows (on display) and board games (hidden inside the cabinet).

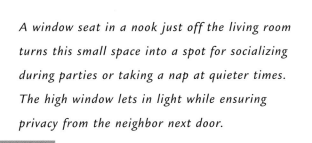

A window seat in a nook just off the living room turns this small space into a spot for socializing during parties or taking a nap at quieter times. The high window lets in light while ensuring privacy from the neighbor next door.

In warmer climates, sometimes the goal is to completely eliminate the barriers between indoors and out. Here, glass accordion doors easily slide to the side to open up the living room to an outdoor patio.

A wall of windows provides views and light. Another wall supports floor-to-ceiling shelves for books and keepsakes, supports a ladder to the attic, and even features a small fireplace that's as much a piece of art as the sculpted head beneath it.

Built-in shelves and cabinets flanking the fireplace provide lots of storage—some hidden, some open—in this cozy living room abutting a kitchen. Helping to delineate the two spaces are a stone-clad counter and a decorative column that hides ceiling supports.

Built-in storage in a living room (right) shows off blue and white vases and bowls through glass-panel doors. Understated drawers below accommodate cutlery, placemats, and other table accessories. Nearby, an airy display case (below) holds mostly clear-glass collectibles, allowing people in other parts of the house to see into the living room.

Keeping furniture choices simple —armless chair, sedan chair, coffee table—makes this small space appealingly cozy. It is also hardworking: the coffee table has multiple shelves below for the inevitable clutter of too many coffee-table books.

living large | open ceiling + open floor plan = big space

The existing open ceiling of this one-story house was only the first step on the road to roominess. The collar ties that span the rafters were also raised, and everything was painted white to further the feeling of airiness. As a final touch, French doors and a row of windows above them were installed to connect the great room to the garden and ensure that the space would routinely be flooded with light.

Kitchens are the nerve centers of most homes, so it just makes good sense to carve out some space for a small family communications hub, as has been done below. This nook just off the kitchen has enough room for a laptop, a reading lamp, and the family phone.

A chest-high partition separates the kitchen from the dining room but still allows conversation. The top of the partition functions as a buffet counter ("order up!") for both family and guests. Shelves built into the bottom half of the partition store cookbooks and special-occasion serving bowls.

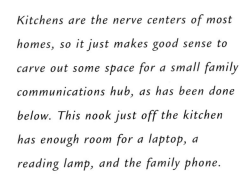

jojo's notebook

bowled over

I've often heard designers refer to long, rectangular rooms as "bowling alleys." They are not being flattering. The owners of this condominium had the additional challenge of making their 30- by 12-foot space function as a kitchen, dining room, and living room.

Luckily, these condo owners are throwing strikes. They dealt with the shape of the space by capitalizing on it. Rectangles show up throughout the long room in the form of the kitchen island, the dining table, even the sofa. Repeating the shape makes the environment appear ordered, calm, and cohesive.

The tall ceiling also does a great job of making the space seem more open, as does the light-giving picture window high up on the room's far wall. Thanks to the space's height, light, and overall balance, this bowling alley has room to spare.

JoJo

When drawn, one of the window coverings becomes a screen for a home theater system

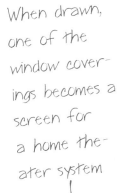

Bertoia chair

A trio of pendant lights fills the void between ceiling and floor without using a lot of space

Backless stools allow the eye to take in everything without interruption

Repeating rectangular shapes in key furnishings maintains design cohesion and demarcates living, dining, and kitchen areas

Counter seating is integrated into the design of this kitchen. Formaldehyde-free wheatboard cabinets are an environmentally conscious, "green" touch. A space-saving microwave oven above the stovetop keeps the counter free for meal prep, while numerous plugs in the tile backsplash permit work to happen where it needs to.

kitchens

The perfect kitchen is not necessarily large, but it is well thought out. The goal, as any chef worth her kosher salt will tell you, is to be able to perform tasks with as little unnecessary motion as possible.

Europeans, who are generally more familiar with small living spaces than Americans, are geniuses when it comes to designing compact but sophisticated kitchens. They know, for example, that a single large sink is more practical than dual sinks. Their kitchens are filled with appliance garages for stowing toasters, mixers, and blenders out of sight, as well as cabinets tucked into odd spaces and outfitted with vertical slats for lids, cookie sheets, oven racks, and trays.

Another strategy is to display rather than store serving trays, special glassware, and china—a wall or open shelf that holds such items is both functional and artistic. And be demanding of the cabinet space you do have. Corner cabinets, often a graveyard for seldom-used pots and pans, are far more functional when outfitted with a lazy-Susan shelf.

This tight space is well served by a four-burner stovetop mounted atop a table that looks like a retrofitted piece of furniture from a home office. A rollaway shelving unit underneath corrals cooking oils and the like.

This long view of the kitchen pictured at left shows how it spills into the living room, separated only by a half-wall that breaks up but doesn't spoil the sight lines from one room to another.

In keeping with the loft-style design of the rest of the house, this kitchen forsakes traditional cabinets and turns a salvaged sink, exposed plumbing, and commercial-grade shelving and appliances into pieces of art. Photographs prominently displayed in the kitchen echo the industrial aesthetic favored by the homeowner.

This window-lined niche breaks through the wall line in the kitchen, pushing a new dining area out into the yard. Floorboard heaters beneath the benches keep the light-filled space cozy in winter.

Chrome fountain stools and a high, narrow table on casters take up little space in this small, traditional kitchen. Remove the chairs and the table can function as a mobile work surface, especially useful for entertaining.

There's not a lot of space in this kitchen, which shares its small footprint with a dining counter and the living room—in fact, kitchen storage spills over into the living room. Fortunately, galvanized bins on open shelves against the wall present an attractive solution.

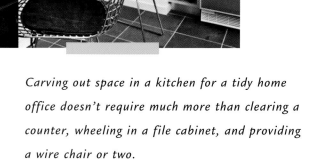

Carving out space in a kitchen for a tidy home office doesn't require much more than clearing a counter, wheeling in a file cabinet, and providing a wire chair or two.

Open views and access to the dining area help make this pocket kitchen feel a bit larger, as does the simple cabinetry.

The narrow width of this kitchen is offset by its generous length, which creates lots of counter space. Even more helpful in de-emphasizing the narrowness of the room is the playful dining area at the far end. Built-in seating and invigorating color make the most of the space.

An updated country farmhouse kitchen utilizes built-ins to store and display coffee mugs, yellow plates, and several stacks of cookbooks. Though space is tight, the cook who rules this kitchen has created a work area for the mixer. Above the stove, a country-style façade hides the vent hood and fan.

A stainless steel–topped breakfast bar and high seats are perfect for casual dining or visiting with guests during meal preparation. Open shelving stores and displays glasses, dry-goods containers, and an assortment of mixing bowls. With the dining table just steps away, the result is one welcoming, integrated room.

A low-rising partition separates a kitchen from a living room and provides a home for the sink, a trash compactor, a microwave, and cookbooks. The combination of natural light and shared space creates an open, friendly environment.

Walls that turn at odd angles often create wedges of underutilized space. Here the designer simply allowed the counter to follow the wall lines (right), then echoed the effect with a high-tech breakfast nook (below) that comfortably seats five in a very small area.

A pull-out drawer gets the most out of the space beneath a stovetop and ensures that pots and lids are conveniently at hand. The shallow translucent cabinet to the left of the stove is both handsome and practical—spices, oils, and condiments are all within easy reach.

Built-in appliances are the key to this efficient European-style kitchen. Instead of taking up valuable counter space, a stainless steel cappuccino machine is mounted in the wall above a microwave—leaving room for a flat-panel computer that lets you catch up on e-mail while dinner is cooking.

floored | wood connects kitchen island to dining area

This kitchen island blends seamlessly into its surrounding space because of the liberal use of Jatoba wood. Naturally water-resistant, the Brazilian hardwood wraps up the side of the island, continues on the countertop, and is even echoed on a far counter and backsplash. The island features a handful of shelves for a message center and a wider section of counter where family or friends can pull up stools for food or conversation.

From the kitchen, the same cooking island pictured on the facing page reveals its harder-working side. There's lots of storage room here, plus a cooktop with an oven below. One thoughtful touch is the open space at the near end of the island—a good place for kids to toss their backpacks when they get home from school and head for the fridge.

Large paneled windows in this dining area roll up and out of sight under eaves that shelter an adjoining deck—explaining why the table is on wheels and ringed by deck chairs. Additional natural-light sources are a room-wide row of clerestory windows and a slender floor-to-ceiling window in the far corner.

Lots of kitchen cabinets these days are built with glass doors, but the cabinet to the left of the classic chrome-and-enamel stove in this kitchen also has a glass back, letting both light and scenery stream in.

The drawer pulls on the cabinets in this long and narrow kitchen give the room a streamlined, racetrack-like perspective that draws the eye to an informal dining area, where a "paddock" of wheat grass grows on a windowsill. Fixtures below and above the cabinets on the left provide direct and indirect illumination.

Sometimes "finding" space can be as simple as mounting an unframed blackboard to a section of unused wall. This kitchen chalkboard is used for shopping lists and family messages. Display shelves on the dining-area side of the island present a decorative face to guests.

In this kitchen corner, cooking utensils are grouped in butter crocks, knives are safely stowed in a butcher-block holder, and cutlery and small appliances are easy to find on commercial-grade shelves beneath the counter. Below, a restaurant-style pot rack is used to separate a kitchen from the dining area; it also stores wine and glasses.

An appliance garage keeps a food
processor accessible but out of sight
when not in use.

A built-in banquette gets maximum seating
out of a tiny corner at the end of this small
kitchen. Shelves above the banquette and
an adjacent picture window run clear to the
ceiling—no wasted space here.

You don't have to carve out a whole lot of counter
space to make room for a modest office area. This
one includes a file cabinet on wheels and slots below
the butcher block for bills and letters.

A collection of brightly colored Fiestaware could have been squirreled away inside wooden cabinets, but its owner chose instead to put it on display on a simple but handsome restaurant storage rack.

This kitchen is literally a dead end that's barely wider than the range and microwave at its terminus. But keeping everything white, from cabinets to appliances to tile counters and backsplash, gives the illusion of more space than is really there.

Sometimes it's not a matter of finding more storage space, just a matter of minimizing what we need to store. By limiting their inventory of plates and glasses, the homeowners were able to make this kitchen feel more open by eliminating bulky cabinets.

The pull-out trash drawer at right works equally well for a quartet of recycling bins, while the addition of a simple wire book-holder at far right frees up counter space for food preparation.

It's easy to get food from the oven to the table when a rustic breakfast bar is just a few feet away. Piano stools, which are space-savers to begin with, can be stored beneath the table when not in use.

Open cabinets provide as much storage space as closed ones, which would have overwhelmed this tiny space. The modest counter offers its cook an additional work surface, and diners a place to eat and converse.

Islands are normally considered luxuries in small kitchens, but here a modest center island provides much-needed counter space and a casual place for a quick breakfast or dinner for two. Note how the island's outer edges are within the kitchen footprint, keeping traffic flow beyond the kitchen unimpeded.

Interior and exterior walls surrounding this jewel-box of a kitchen were replaced with large glass panes, removing visual barriers to the dining room and backyard deck. Pots and pans hang above the island, which is where guests like to hang out before, during, and after dinner parties.

Since it's so much a part of the adjacent dining and living areas, this open and airy kitchen has to look good. That's why the shelves to the right of the stove are as much about display as they are about storage.

Wooden dowels secured to a metal base make it easy to get the maximum amount of storage for a collection of Japanese flatware and bowls.

A clever and safe way to store valuable plates is to stand them on their sides in a single drawer divided with dowels.

This casual seating area, just off the kitchen, demands little space but commands lots of attention with red and yellow chairs that stand out handsomely against a purple wall.

The red I-beam brings this kitchen up to earthquake code, but neither design nor storage suffers as a result of the intrusion. If anything, the division in the cabinet at the beam's base illustrates how a so-called imperfection can be transformed into a focal point.

open plan | creating spaciousness with height and light

Walls or partitions would have destroyed the loftlike feel of this rustic, relatively narrow vacation home. The kitchen is simply a part of a single open room, which means that whoever is cooking can benefit from the barn doors that slide into the wall to open the entire area to views of the beach. The high ceiling adds volumes to the sense of spaciousness.

From the kitchen, the other end of the house appears focused on a fireplace. Most of the seating and all of the cabinets are built in, so only a few other pieces of furniture are required to make family and friends comfortable. Outdoor-type light fixtures suspended from the ceiling make the clutter of lamps and tables unnecessary.

treasure island

If you've been searching for kitchen efficiency, this island is a multifunctional find. It's got plenty of work surfaces for dishwashing and food prep, the elevated wooden countertop encourages guests to gather round and socialize, and its numerous storage touches are ingenious.

Check out the channel between the two counters— it holds frequently used items like cereal bowls, coffee cups, and glasses. And don't overlook the paneled column to the right of the dishwasher (see inset at left). This is the sort of space that often goes unused in islands and wall cabinets alike; here it hides a neatly organized spice rack. If your palate shies away from the spicy and savory, a sliver of space like this could easily be configured to handle such kitchen treasures as cookbooks, cutting boards, cookie sheets, or canned goods.

JoJo

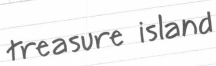

A narrow column on the island's end hides a now-you-see-it-now-you-don't spice rack

This channel of space is perfect for favorite coffee cups and other oft-used items

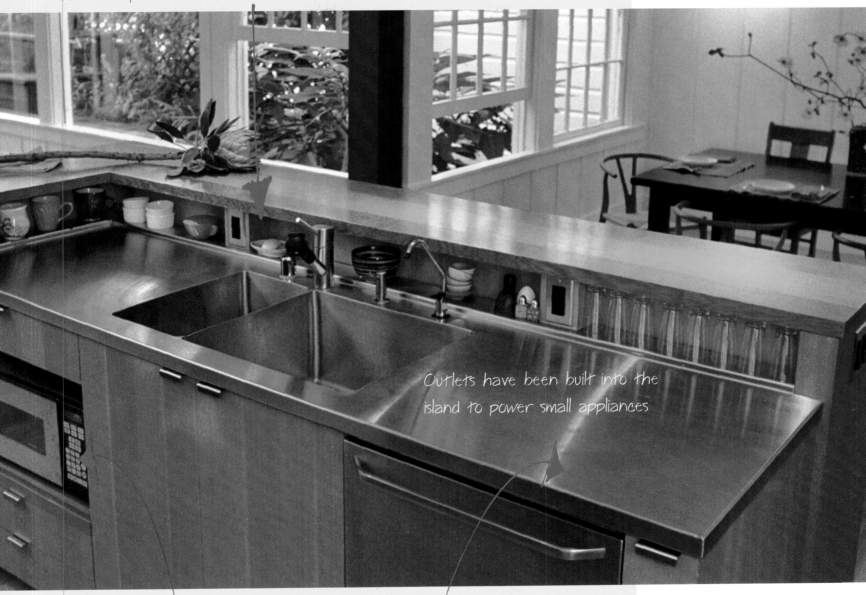

Outlets have been built into the island to power small appliances

Tucking a microwave into the island saves space else- where in the kitchen

The seamless stainless-steel countertop accentuates the island's length and depth

What once was a dark, shallow dining room gets a breathtaking facelift with tall French doors opening to a narrow deck and inviting the outdoors inside. In a nod to the new informality, seating on one side of the table is handled by a single picnic-table-style bench.

dining rooms

For some time now, there's been a trend away from the "formal" dining room, that dark and sequestered place where Grandma's heirloom sideboard stood. These days, the dining room is more likely to be almost an appendage to the kitchen, an inviting spot not only for eating meals but also for perusing the newspaper, doing homework, playing cards, or sewing a costume for the school play.

Because of its proximity to the kitchen, this room just naturally draws everyone for one activity or another. So it's important to make it useful. Flow, proportion, and efficiency make a good small-space dining room. That means keeping it open, with a transparent transition to the kitchen or the living room, or both. Someone who's chopping vegetables should be able to have a conversation with whoever is leafing through a magazine on the sofa.

A single built-in cabinet against one wall can act as serving surface as well as store your better glassware, silverware, and dinnerware. Shallow lower shelves for placemats, napkins, and serving trays make it easy to set a table without interfering with traffic in the kitchen.

And consider architectural elements to set the dining area apart. Lowering the ceiling here can make the space feel more intimate and act as a visual room divider. Spotlights on dimmers let you brighten work surfaces when the kids are doing math or soften the mood for a romantic dinner. Blond or light-colored flooring will make the space feel bigger and, like the lowered ceiling, serve as a visual clue that you're in a separate room.

Elegant chairs with woven leather seats and backs, formal tableware and china, and a dark countertop offer a more decorative alternative to the standard breakfast bar.

Sometimes dining areas have to do more than seat four for dinner. In small houses, they often double as a place for items that would be stored in the kitchens of larger dwellings. Here, open shelving for dishes and glassware is built into two walls.

A round formal table and six chairs fill this dining space. It works because other than some art on the wall, there's nothing to clutter up the room (even the sideboard is small). But what really makes the room are pocket French doors that slide open to allow access to a garden.

Defining a dining area in a larger open room can be as simple as adding to a kitchen island. Here, a row of open shelves atop the island subtly divides the kitchen from the dining area—the decorative storage space houses a collection of ornamental ceramics and glass.

Benches against a wall and beneath wood-framed windows offer comfortable seating for casual meals; chairs on the near side of the table are largely out of the room's traffic areas. Drawers below the benches provide secret storage compartments for little-used items.

Rather than hiding these ceramic vases and plates in storage drawers beneath the built-in bench, the homeowners have put them on display like pieces of art. Shelving above a window, as seen here, is an easy way to squeeze just a little bit more storage space out of a small room.

One way to maximize space is to minimize furniture size. This built-in dining table is anchored against built-in cabinets and supported by a single wrought-iron leg.

Location is everything, they say. This dining island's proximity to a computer and office area makes it a natural spot not only for getting a bite to eat but also for paying bills or getting caught up on one's reading.

A large, framed mirror makes this modest dining area appear much larger. Not only does it visually increase the room's size, it also opens up views of the rest of the house for dinner guests seated facing the wall.

Everything is efficient and high-tech in this modern kitchen, where a stainless steel island is both work counter and dining area. Translucent cabinet doors on either side of the hood-and-shelf unit above the stove seem less massive than opaque doors would, and they reveal contents at a glance.

Most one-room-apartment dwellers forsake a dining area, but in this dorm-size room, a dining table that can double as a desk is crowned with a platform bed supported by industrial shelving.

A half-wall between kitchen and dining area allows an open view between cooks and diners and makes both spaces feel larger. The dining area also benefits from built-in cabinets, which hide dishes and tableware, and a light-filled alcove.

Sliding glass doors, pulled back in good weather, make an outdoor deck feel like a part of this dining space—and the picture window at the table's far end amplifies the illusion. Though not designed for outdoor use, the dining table and chairs suggest outdoor design influences.

visual flow | sight lines open the kitchen to the living room

Many small, older homes are divided into numerous smaller rooms. Where creating a big, open space is simply not an option, you can still enjoy a feeling of spaciousness if traffic flow and sight lines from room to room are as seamless as possible. The large doorway in the foreground of the small house below lets you see from the living room through the dining room and on into the kitchen.

In the kitchen, organization is key. Coffee cups are both out of the way and decorative when they hang on hooks. Above the cups, open shelving serves as a grid for plates and dishes organized by size, type, and color. Glassware stays dust-free behind glass-panel cabinets. And the sink commands a place of prominence in the kitchen's sunny corner, ensuring that whoever is toiling there can see people in the rest of the house.

To the right of the sink, the open shelves above the coffee cups are repeated in a smaller version; a void above the shelves leaves room for a ram's skull, echoing the animal theme of artwork throughout the house. A 27-inch integrated refrigerator is hidden behind the cabinetry to the right of the mixer.

jojo's notebook

dining room dq

There are rooms that wow you with their wild colors and radical patterns, and then there are rooms like this one that dazzle with their superior DQ ("design quotient"). The secret is a balanced composition of furniture, textures, and accessories, as well as a warm, neutral palette. For example, the highly polished wood surfaces are elegant, while the woven textures are casual. The decision to cover only two of the five chairs to create a bit of deliberate asymmetry suggests a design that doesn't take itself too seriously.

The tight room also gets high marks for its smart use of space. Round tables have long been a staple of small dining spaces—you can typically seat more people at a 48-inch round table than at a comparably sized square or rectangular one. Below the window is a built-in seat, and below that a hand-some, open cabinet holds books and decorating accessories.

JoJo

An area rug helps define the space; woven jute and bamboo are especially affordable

Coordinating the light fixture with the table in shape and color creates continuity

Rather than being hidden behind curtains or shades, the mullions are left exposed

Storage below the window seat is open, so it recedes away instead of closing in on the room

Slip-covering just two of the chairs prevents texture overload

Accordion panels, open on top and bottom, provide a measure of privacy in a bedroom that shares space with the rest of an open-plan dwelling. Translucent glass brightens the room. Lights are positioned only where needed, while a small table mounted to the platform at the foot of the bed offers a surface for books without impinging on the room's dimensions, or the sleeper.

bedrooms

Your bedroom is the most important room in the house—more so than your living room, bathroom, or even kitchen. Regardless of its size, it's the room where you ought to feel most comfortable.

What makes a small room comfortable? It's all about organization. Clutter is stressful—ask any parent who has ever walked into her teenager's bedroom. The good news is that you don't need a lot of space to be organized. A floor-to-ceiling shelf only 18 inches wide, with shelves spaced every 6 inches, can hold dozens of shoes. Drawers or shallow storage boxes beneath the bed are perfect for linens, hats, even wrapping paper.

A few key creature comforts can take your bedroom from the realm of merely comfortable to downright cozy. Luxurious bed linens don't take any more space than more ordinary products, while a few well-placed works of art, some family photos, and a good lamp next to a reading chair complete the relaxing picture.

An MP3 player docked into a set of speakers takes up hardly any room on a bedside table, yet it brings the equivalent of a full stereo system to this small bedroom.

Sometimes tight quarters are exactly right for a bedroom. This tiny guest bed, for example, is squeezed into an equally tiny nook, giving the lucky visitor who sleeps here the feeling of being in a small cabin or bunkhouse.

An unused closet was converted into an alcove for bunk beds, allowing this guest room to accommodate four people instead of just two. Curtains mounted to the wall above the former closet can be closed when the bunks are not in use.

Rather than display vases, travel mementos, and family photos on furniture that would crowd this small room, the owner of this charming bedroom decided to place these objects on floor-to-ceiling shelves flanking the head of a bed. Halogen spotlights make more than a single accessory lamp unnecessary.

Simple but very practical, a modest dining table with slat chairs fits in perfectly with a low platform bed that steals some of its space from a former closet. The white wall, broken only by a small window, is left unadorned to keep the small room from feeling too busy.

Some bedrooms work best when their divisions from other areas are clearly defined yet free of doors. In this bedroom, featuring built-in bedside tables and shelves supporting a modest collection of blown glass, the seating area inside a walk-in closet is in plain sight, as is a small library and work area.

There wasn't much space beneath this wide window overlooking a bamboo garden—just enough to squeeze in a guest bed that faces a flat-panel TV.

Murphy beds are terrific solutions for home offices that must occasionally serve as guest rooms, but not all are as handsome as this one. The decorative woodworking on this bed's "wall" side makes what lies behind it that much more of a surprise.

Kids love a fun, cozy sleeping area, accomplished here by means of cloth curtains on a ceiling track. The curtains are usually open during the day to make the room feel larger, then closed at night for privacy (and to keep monsters at bay).

This children's bedroom takes its cue from playground equipment. Beds are at different heights, for crawling around, with storage beneath them. The oval opening at right is the entrance to a short slide that drops kids into a play and reading area separated from sleeping areas by a fortlike façade.

Bunk beds are the original space-saver for kids' rooms. The large bedroom in the vacation home at left features a pair of bunks. Anchoring their ends to nonbearing walls created space for desk-like seating areas on the opposite sides. Below, color-coded bunk beds are tucked into niches and situated at different heights to create cozy berths. There's even room for toys underneath.

Favorite books are neatly organized in a simple shelving unit that also includes a partner's reading desk. Wooden stools can be stowed beneath the desk when not in use.

peaceful perch | build out to expand your horizons

The sleeping nook shown here and on the facing page is a contemporary take on the old-fashioned sleeping porch. Large windows topped by unobtrusive pull-down shades make the room seem to float at treetop level, offering unimpeded views of the neighborhood. An unbroken pane of glass above the wide doorway lets light pass into the adjacent room; the absence of a door between the room and the nook ensures seamless flow between the two. Drawers under the built-in platform bed store pillows and blankets.

Glass encloses the nook on its three exterior sides, one of which features a sliding window for fresh air. Particularly ingenious is the use of an uninterrupted pane of glass for the near wall, heightening the nook's sense of openness.

The nook is perched over a landing that's about halfway up from the street. As such, it's at once a public and a private space—high enough from the street for peace and quiet, yet close enough to the stairway and the home's entrance to have a public dimension.

The idea of the kitchen island is well understood, that of a closet island less so. Here, the back of a freestanding closet serves as the bed's headboard. The closet's L shape defines a dressing area, while built-in cabinets at the island's near end keep the rest of the room free of space-hogging furniture.

This airy bedroom would feel much smaller without its tall panel of windows and the glass door opening to an outside seating area. The spare lines of a single wooden chair are similarly open and airy, making the chair seem to take up little space.

Translucent floor-to-ceiling panels let in lots of light and suggest what's on the other side while still preserving privacy in this bedroom. A louvered window above the bed provides both privacy and air circulation.

Beds can be tucked into
the oddest little spaces.
This daybed looks perfectly
at home below a flight
of stairs—and a trundle
beneath it provides an
additional mattress for
a child's friends or out-
of-town guests.

Except for narrow paths on either side of the double
bed, this cozy attic guest room is entirely taken up by
its sleeping surface.

The sloping ceiling line in this attic bedroom seems to shelter the head of the room's main bed. A built-in daybed against the window can be offered to guests or used during the day for reading or studying, and it provides storage space below.

This sports fan's knotty-pine bedroom includes an office area at the foot of the bed. The built-in armchairs that flank the desk have storage compartments underneath, as do the bed and the built-in closet.

Part of a detached guest cottage
that used to be a garage, this small
bedroom had no room for a flight
of stairs. Instead, a space-saving
ladder leads to a small storage
space in the attic.

Replacing a hinged bathroom door with a hanging
one that slides along a rail yielded more floor
space for the adjacent bedroom. The translucent
windows set into the corner of the interior wall
help both of these small rooms feel larger.

Some climates permit porches to double as bedrooms. During balmy weather, the owners of this cabinlike house can pull down their outside Murphy bed and "camp out" on a deck that extends from a bedroom.

The entire wall of this Los Angeles home opens up like a garage door so that someone lying in bed can look out on the tropical garden just beyond. Inside, bookshelves are squeezed in at the foot of the bed and above a nightstand as a sculptural element.

short commute | an office that's at home in a bedroom

At first glance, this bedroom seems rather typical—suspended bookcase on the wall, simple built-in dresser for clothes, small desk in the middle. On closer examination it becomes clear that this is not just a bedroom but also a fully functional home office. Yet even though the room has to do much more than provide a place to sleep, it still feels like a bedroom.

While the low closet on the right was designed to hold shirts on hangers,
it also has room for the computer tower that's connected to a keyboard
and monitor on the desk. Tucking the phone beneath the desk but within
easy grasp frees up even more space.

jojo's notebook

sheer delight

Strip away everything in this combination bedroom, dining room, and living area and you're left with an L-shaped room with a large picture window and parquet floors. Not exactly awe-inspiring, but after some design sleight of hand, it's become a cool little hideaway.

Few furnishings or accessories have been used, yet the room feels polished and alive. Natural light pouring through the window travels unobstructed through a sheer curtain and a pair of acrylic chairs. Meanwhile, the geometric grid of the parquet is contrasted with sassy patterns over the bed and in artwork above the small table for two.

But it's that flimsy curtain separating the sleeping area from the rest of the room that, ironically, works the hardest. Running it from the floor to the ceiling helps elongate the rest of the space. It's all part of the minimal-furniture-for-maximum-effect aesthetic that makes this lean pad so mean.

JoJo

This soft, sexy divider is a simple project for sew-it-yourselfers

Bold color works well in groups, and in small doses

Vertically stacking three small paintings creates a big visual impact

Clear acrylic chairs are almost invisible

Slender metal legs reduce the mass of this table

The custom-designed bathroom cabinet on the left eliminates the need for additional storage underneath a sink set into a glass counter. Plumbing is hidden, but not obsessively so, by a rack for towels. The result is an open design that makes the room feel clean and airy.

bathrooms

Here's an amazing fact: on average, each of us spends three years of our life in the bathroom. Along with your bedroom, this is the most intimate space in your house, a place where you really should sweat the small stuff.

Start at the bottom with heated floors, a relatively small investment ($600 to $800 for an average-size bathroom) with a big payoff. And make sure your cabinets work as hard as they should. Cabinet drawers with built-in outlets keep hair dryers, curling irons, and electric toothbrushes off the countertop. Line other drawers with special trays for lipsticks, nail polishes, or hair ornaments. Purchase plastic dividers to organize vitamins, prescription medicines, ointments.

Seriously consider the ways in which you use your bathroom. If you almost never take a bath (people with whirlpool tubs use them an average of four times a year), do you really need a large bathtub? Multifunctional showers—some with steam, aromatherapy, and even full-body hydro-massage—take up no more room than normal showers. If you prefer tub baths, consider a deep, narrow soaker that consumes a much smaller footprint than a traditional tub.

The vivid green color of this wall, which takes its cue from the chartreuse interior of the bowl-shaped sink, gives a serene feel to a small bathroom.

Glass is the key to the open feeling of this bathroom. The glass wall separating the shower from the platform tub lets natural light into the shower and on through to the rest of the room, thanks to the glass shower door.

A second view of the shower to the left reveals a mosaic-tile-covered niche for storing bath amenities. The tile bench gives bathers a place to relax during a shower or while drying off, taking advantage of all the natural light.

A small soaking pool is built into a bathroom niche, giving it a private view out into the garden. Placing the spa in a niche frees up the rest of the bathroom floor space.

A simple shelf steals space beneath a sloping roof and continues over a vanity. The mirror extends into the skylight, higher than needed for shaving or putting on makeup but a good way to reflect much-needed light into this small and enclosed bathroom.

A slender, slat-sided tower eliminates the need to store towels in a separate linen closet. The towels are hidden from general view by being positioned right where they are needed most.

One towel-storage option is to use the space below the sink. This single open shelf has been built out of heavy industrial-grade metal in a deliberate and clever bit of over-designing.

An outdoor shower and a round tub are tucked under this home's eaves. Privacy is achieved by means of blinds that rise only as high as decorum requires.

There's not much room here, but having the ceiling rise up to the rafters makes this bathroom feel a lot more spacious than its narrow footprint suggests. This visual trick is echoed in the shape of the shower window, which parallels the roofline.

The intimate setting for this claw-foot bathtub could not feel more relaxing. The peaked ceiling line defines the space below it; a skylight set into the ceiling's slope seems to spotlight the tub. To maintain the clean look, the tub plumbing was installed in the floor and wall framing.

Two small, open vanities share a towel cabinet with frosted-glass front; his and hers medicine chests flank the matching mirrors. The use of small ceramic mosaic tiles on the floor adds texture and color without overpowering the room.

Cantilevered shelves made of high-grade plywood act as an informal divider between the vanity and the toilet without obstructing light from the window. The shelves are used primarily for decorative objects, a luxury in bathrooms of almost any size.

If you live in a warm climate, one solution to the problem of a tiny bathroom might be to take your shower outdoors. A shower curtain, anchored at the top and corners to keep it from flapping in the breeze, provides all the privacy this space needs.

A freestanding glass sink keeps things simple in this bathroom, where a custom-built divider with shelves at unpredictable angles provides fanciful storage. The divider also creates a barrier between the sink and the toilet.

Taking advantage of the space in a slanted niche above a toilet was mandatory in this small bathroom. The owner not only decided to store towels here, she decided to use only vivid red ones—simultaneously solving a storage problem and making a strong design statement.

A large sliding glass door at the far end of a cedar Japanese soaking tub lets in lots of light while providing a terrific view of a private garden. Built-in shelves below the sink echo the lines of the wood that sheathes the walls and covers the floor.

Placed in a sunlit corner of a master bathroom, this European-style soaking tub takes advantage of corner windows that give bathers the illusion of being up in the trees. The sloped ceiling hits its lowest point close to the tub, creating a sense of enclosure that feels welcome here, not confining.

now you see it... | swinging wall divides bed and bath

In this house, if you sat up in bed and looked behind the headboard you'd see this efficient little bathroom—at least when the upper part of the bed cabinetry is swung open. Storage over the toilet is built into the same cabinetry that supports a sink. A skylight over the shower, which is entered through the glass door to the right, illuminates both bathroom and bedroom when the partition is open.

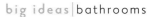

When the cabinetry above the headboard is opened (a track in the ceiling helps it swing easily), it becomes a half-wall in the bathroom on the other side. The headboard itself, with its books and lighting, remains above the bed. Opening up the space like this makes both sides feel a bit bigger. Closing the swinging cabinet gives both rooms more privacy.

Immediately on the other side of the headboard is a deep, one-person soaking tub. Someone using the tub can choose either an intimate experience or one that benefits from light streaming in through the bedroom's floor-to-ceiling windows.

jojo's notebook

bathed in perfection

This recently remodeled bathroom is generous with amenities but downright miserly about wasting space. Foremost among its numerous space-saving ideas is the pocket door that slides unobtrusively in and out of a wall cavity (the average pocket door, I'm told, saves up to 9 square feet of space over a traditional swinging door). One of the main storage features, a wall cabinet (left), has been recessed and wired with electrical receptacles so that unattractive appliances like blow dryers, curling irons, and electric razors can be charged and stored out of sight.

By saving a square foot here and a few inches there, the owners of this bathroom had enough space left over for a large, luxurious shower (inset above) with multiple shower heads and a built-in seat. The frameless glass surround and white subway tiles enhance the bright, open feeling.

JoJo

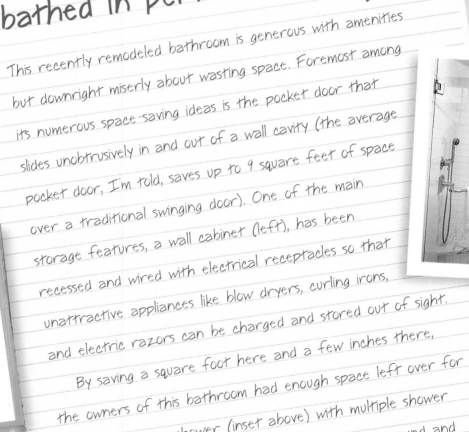

An outlet in a cabinet allows you to charge devices without taking up counter space

This pocket door was designed to slide across an arched doorway

The rich espresso finish on the cabinetry is a warm contrast to all the white

White subway tile in the shower and a basket-weave design on the floor lend a nostalgic air

Pushing right up against the edges of this house, a small office tucked beneath a sloping ceiling provides plenty of room for books and lots of desk space. Spotlights eliminate the need for space-hogging desk lamps, while the choice of the laptop computer seems as much of a design decision here as it is a technical one.

home offices

The den, that room where Ward talked to Wally and the Beav when the boys got into trouble, has long since been replaced by the home office for today's families. In some cases this space is dedicated solely to taking care of business (particularly if you're asking the IRS for a write-off). But more often, the home office is a multi-functional room where bills are paid, homework is researched, and household records—from title certificates to appliance warranties—are stored. A small LCD TV, tucked on a shelf, allows personal viewing of movies or TV shows. Better yet, many computer monitors obviate the need for a separate TV altogether.

Got guests? A futon or a small daybed is perfectly compatible with most home offices. Or install a Murphy bed to give you more floor space—a generous circulation area always makes a small room feel larger.

If you don't have a dedicated room in your house for a home office, considering pressing a closet into service. Closets can be transformed into gift-wrapping headquarters, sewing nooks, or craft centers for scrapbooking, printing family photos, or editing vacation videos.

This office in the transition space between two rooms features a desk that's only as deep as the wall to its left; it makes up for its shallow depth by being extremely wide.

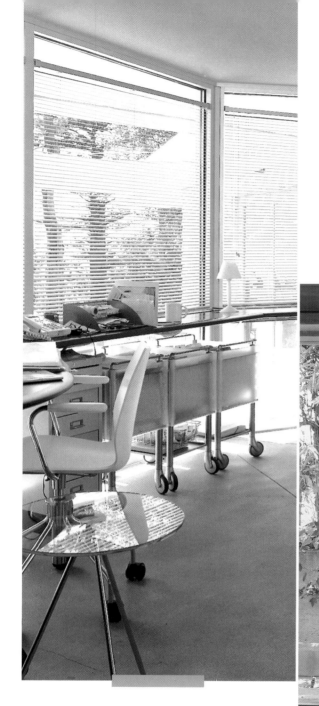

A built-in desk running along the wall, a couple of rolling carts, and a chair make for an almost invisible office in a room that has other uses as well.

Rather than facing a wall, this small home office resembling an oversize window box looks out on the garden. Not framing the glass at its two right angles on the left eliminates visual barriers between interior and exterior spaces, making the room feel a bit bigger.

An oddly angled space just off the living room and kitchen becomes the perfect student homework center. Shelves on the lower part of the Japanese-style cabinet are open for easy access, while the higher shelves have sliding doors to keep the look from being too cluttered.

A tall desk lamp, a desktop bookcase, a blackboard for family messages—there's a lot going on here in a small space, but using a laptop and a stool instead of a chair keeps things from feeling crowded.

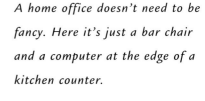

A home office doesn't need to be fancy. Here it's just a bar chair and a computer at the edge of a kitchen counter.

This is a very busy space, but it's serving the needs of two very busy people. The drawers between the chairs and a printing center on the counter define and separate the workstations. In this case, shelves were left open because instant access to books was the most important factor.

An industrial shelving unit on heavy-duty casters is an excellent storage solution for books and periodicals—less expensive than installed cabinets and more flexible (as your office area evolves, your books can move wherever you need them to go).

This architect's work space is tucked under one end of a gable roof. A built-in desk and a broad ledge frame the room and offer lots of work surface. Natural light from a skylight washes the walls, giving the room the feel of a treehouse.

Neatly labeled cardboard boxes can be stacked to organize bills or, as in this example, hobby materials—proving that storage boxes needn't be unsightly. An old-fashioned picture light doubles as the light source for the desk.

This small closet better served its owners by being converted into a home office. The door was the first thing to go. Then cabinets were installed above and below the desk—the flat-panel computer screen and tuck-away keyboard tray are concessions to the desk's shallow depth.

There's not much unused space beneath these stairs. Drawers to the right and a narrow shelving unit for collectibles to the left flank an efficient home office. The phone has been mounted on the wall so it doesn't take up space on the crowded desk.

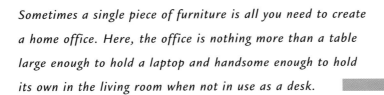

Sometimes a single piece of furniture is all you need to create a home office. Here, the office is nothing more than a table large enough to hold a laptop and handsome enough to hold its own in the living room when not in use as a desk.

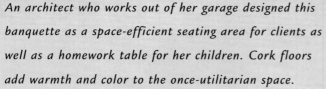

An architect who works out of her garage designed this banquette as a space-efficient seating area for clients as well as a homework table for her children. Cork floors add warmth and color to the once-utilitarian space.

A small, stand-alone home office is separated from the rest of the house by a brilliant flower garden. Large windows and architectural echoes (in this case, the sloping walls) unite the two spaces.

A built-in desk and open storage cabinets run under the dormer windows of this second-floor home office, part of a larger room that also encompasses the home's living and dining areas.

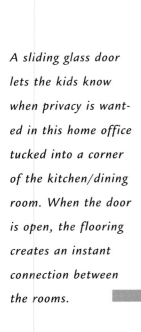

A sliding glass door lets the kids know when privacy is wanted in this home office tucked into a corner of the kitchen/dining room. When the door is open, the flooring creates an instant connection between the rooms.

home work | an office where you can sleep on the job

The most common combination room is probably the home office that is occasionally pressed into duty as a guest room. Making guests feel welcome is important, of course, but so is a

steady paycheck, so make sure your combo room works first and foremost as an office. This one features spectacular floor-to-ceiling windows—wisely, the couple who share the space work with their backs to the view or they might not get anything done.

The desk in the photo on the facing page disappears when a queen-size Murphy bed folds down and the office becomes a guest room. The table does not have to be stowed separately because it collapses when the bed is pulled out from the wall.

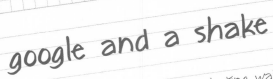

jojo's notebook

google and a shake

It's easy to imagine a roller-skating waitress serving burgers and shakes in this '50s-inspired dining area. What's not so easy to imagine is e-mailing, shopping on eBay, and Googling in this same space. Beyond the funky colors and nostalgic decor, this dinette is all business. The movable cart adjacent to the booth (left) houses a computer workstation. Its proximity to the banquette transforms the booth into a colorful corner office.

The idea of a '50s diner juxtaposed with 21st-century technology is imaginative and cheeky, but it's also practical. That said, I probably would have put the brakes on the sheer volume of accessories—with all those exposed dishes and commercial artworks looming over me, I don't know how I'd get any work done. I'd bet you could pare down the visuals by about half without diluting the room's peachy-keen '50s flavor.

JoJo

Hanging files and hardware such as a scanner are hidden inside this cart

Open-faced shelves store and display dishes

The corner table maximizes seating without crowding the room, and there's still space for a laptop

Its bright red wheels permit this fanciful file cabinet to be moved about the room as work demands

To create a private corner in this backyard, the owners mounted blue-hued translucent corrugated plastic panels, purchased from a home improvement center, on a standard redwood fence. The addition of a few fold-up canvas chairs and a moveable firepit completed the conversion of the space into a cozy outdoor conversation area.

transition spaces

In real estate, it's all about the square footage of your house, condo, or apartment. But it shouldn't be. Properly utilized, the areas immediately around your abode are just as important as the rooms inside, which makes the transition spaces that bridge the two more important still.

Even with minimal space, you can make interior rooms feel larger by making the outdoors part of your view. French doors opening onto nothing more than a 3-foot-wide deck at least open onto something. It's not the space itself that makes the room feel so much larger but the light the French doors admit and the view that draws your eye beyond the room. And if that view includes an awesome little garden with potted citrus and planters of herbs, miniature vegetables, and bright perennials, then so much the better.

Porches and sunrooms are two more examples of transition areas that make a home feel larger. A roofed porch can offer a pleasant breakfast nook or a place to enjoy an end-of-the-day cocktail. Consider your entry stairs and landings too. Cladding them in slate, brick, or Mexican pavers that complement the decor inside can visually extend your home's interior entry area.

Extending off the house and into the yard, this mudroom is a lovely, light-filled place for storing shoes, boots, and towels.

A translucent fireplace surround in this living room replaced a heavy oak-and-marble wall that blocked the light and the views of the canyon below.

Just a few pieces of outdoor furniture are all it takes to turn this sunroom into an inviting spot to sip coffee and read the paper.

A covered porch increases the dimensions of an adjacent sitting room. The sitting room's 12-foot-wide glass doors slide open to take full advantage of the outdoors. A similar space can be created at relatively small expense by building a slim deck under a home's eaves.

An overhead extension helps transform the deck and steps outside a bedroom into an informal sitting area. Walled off from neighbors' view by a row of towering bamboo, the concrete-and-stone patio features an outdoor table that can be used for family dining or entertaining. The nearby fountain provides a bubbling soundtrack.

You don't need a lot of space to create a pleasant sitting area and garden. The patio of this townhouse became its own little room with the addition of just a few signature plants, a couple of containers, and a chair.

al fresco | prefab living at its most gracious

Seamless access to outdoor spaces can be the key to making small interior spaces livable—in warm climates, you really owe it to yourself to take full advantage of the outdoors. As a case in point, every room in the Sunset® Breezehouse™, a modernist prefab, opens to the outside. Here, the master bedroom and a family room off the home's breezeway share a deck and an outdoor dining area. Some doors slide open and others swing out, leaving interior spaces free.

The kitchen of the prefab shown on the facing page opens onto the same breezeway and also onto a second, smaller outdoor living/dining area built of fiberglass-backed natural slate squares that attach to the deck joists. Clerestory windows contribute to the breezeway's sense of airiness. Notice how the kitchen's corner doors have the same orientation as the bedroom's.

big concepts
maxing your space

floor plans ❀ design elements ❀ sight lines ❀ color ❀ height
❀ light ❀ architectural tricks ❀ bonus spaces ❀ getting organized

floor plans

Flexibility is the key to maximizing limited floor space. Portable, hinged dividers made out of everything from paper products to hardwoods can act as privacy screens and temporary partitions, allowing you to split a fair-size room into both bedroom and home office without having to add walls. Easier still is to arrange furniture so that, say, the back of couch acts as a low wall.

Sometimes the extra space we're looking for is already there—we just don't see it. A little-used alcove can become a compact home office with the addition of a fold-up cabinet built into the wall. A secretary desk in the dining room or family room can become a bill-paying center. It's not always about how much space we have but, more importantly, how we use that space.

The furniture in this 850-square-foot house acts as room dividers. The L-shaped couch separates the family room/entertainment area from the dining room, while a small table on wheels can shift position to become either a work surface or part of the informal dining area.

A see-through curtain gives this bedroom a sense of separation. When space is this tight (this bedroom must share space with a dining area), you need to use every trick in the book—like translucent saucer chairs that seem to take hardly any space at all.

A built-in storage partition and shelving unit not only separates the dining room from the living area, it also hides the entrance to a bedroom. Taking the partition all the way up to the slanted open-beam ceiling would have produced too bulky a look, as well as needlessly disrupting the room's open floor plan.

design elements

Sometimes changing an architectural feature—removing a wall, enlarging a room—just isn't practical. Or, ironically, it isn't enough. A design-based feature, however, might produce the same effect. An oversize mirror hung above a fireplace or couch is a relatively simple design element that can make a space feel larger—at the same time inviting peeks into the kitchen, dining room, or other areas reflected in its surface.

Varying ceiling heights is a more radical solution, though the payoff can be well worth it. The sloping ceiling in a living room might shelter a cozy sitting area at its lowest end, then open up the room to the rest of the house at its 12-foot peak. Leaving ceiling beams exposed in any small room tends to make it feel bigger.

Multiple mirrors on the walls of this narrow bathroom seem to double the amount of space. Repeated shapes—dots on the mirrors and holes in the cabinets, small squares in the mosaic tile—are secondary design elements.

A vividly colored plaster wall rising up and into the open-beam ceiling gives this monolith the impact of a painting or a built-in aquarium, except in this case the focal point is an eye-level fireplace. Painting the wall a color that contrasts with the rest of the room leaves no doubt as to where we should turn our attention.

White walls, white shelves, and white built-in cabinets make the space around this dark fireplace feel open, but the main design element here is the stunning mirror over the mantle. No mere accent, this grand piece dramatically expands the perceived room dimensions, about doubling the natural light.

Custom cabinetry handcrafted by the talented owner provides the design element in this kitchen. Instead of being hung on a wall, these cabinets are suspended from the ceiling and incorporate lights that illuminate task areas. The woodwork continues along the ceiling in two places to differentiate the kitchen from adjoining rooms.

sight lines

A house just naturally seems larger when you have un-obstructed views into and across various rooms. A view that angles diagonally from a corner of the kitchen, through the dining room, and on to an opposite corner of the family or living room makes a big impact on our perception of the space. It is as if we are looking at one large room, perhaps divided only by a low counter or a piece of furniture, instead of a series of small, boxy rooms enclosed by walls.

Long hallways, which are often a colossal waste of space, present great opportunities to literally enlarge a house. Using a low wall instead to separate a family or living room from a hallway leading to adjacent rooms makes living spaces feel larger because we are able to move about visually, something that psychologically makes us feel like there's more "there" there. A similar idea can be used in the kitchen. Instead of backing up an appliance like a stove against a solid wall, blocking your sight line into the adjoining room, consider a partition that's only as high as the appliance itself.

Open sight lines are especially welcome in kitchens so that the cook can converse with family members or guests. Here, a modest 6-inch backsplash on the edge of the counter is all it takes to suggest a separation between the kitchen and the dining room—without impeding the views between the two.

The little Juliet balcony lets those upstairs see what's happening in the kitchen and dining area below. Conversely, people downstairs can call up to the balcony to direct stragglers to head down for dinner. Also helpful are the views down the halls on either side of the home's central core.

color

Think of color as the visual sound track to your home. What mood are you trying to establish in a room? For instance, vivid colors like ginger-lily red or lemon yellow stimulate our senses and heighten our awareness. They can draw our attention to specific design elements in the room, like a collection of orange or green Fiestaware or brilliant-hued Mexican folk art. Using eye-popping colors says, "Here is a room for the stimulation of our senses, not a place to take a nap." Such colors are the equivalent of a fast-paced musical score that makes our heart race.

But color, like music, also evokes emotions in more subtle ways. For example, painting an alcove in a neutral-colored room a darker hue sets it apart and draws us to that space, which feels cozier for the contrast. This is where you go when you want to curl up with a good book. Color can fool us too. A series of rooms unbroken by walls—a living room flowing into a dining room and then the kitchen, for instance—can be delineated by using complementary wall colors that create a forced perspective, making us think the individual rooms are bigger than they are.

And it's not just about wall colors. Light-colored floors also create the sense of uninterrupted space. They become an underlying theme that's repeated throughout the house, amplified by the colors of walls, ceilings, and even furniture.

Sometimes color is used to transform, as in a once-dark hallway that is now a fun thoroughfare (above). At other times color is used to pick up nearby hues—in the kitchen at right, a green wall seems to mimic the lawn outside. The green gets additional punch from a vibrant red counter.

A solid red wall might have felt oppressive here, so a ceiling-to-waist-level opening was created. The shelf at its base holds a single glass bowl, while the space above it invites the eye to look into the adjoining room. The red wall continues above the opening to the dining area.

The deep blue wall at the end of this living room is a dramatic focal point—and a clever counterpoint of solid color to the square outlines of the room's framed windows. Note the kitchen counter in the foreground, evidence of the room's tight dimensions.

height

A low ceiling can make you feel either claustrophobic or cozy; it all depends on where and how it is used. As an example, a large room with a single-level low ceiling can feel oppressive. But by lowering the ceiling over just part of a room—an alcove, a window bench, a breakfast bar, or a small room adjacent to a larger one—you delineate a space in the room and suggest its function.

Varying the height of your ceiling adds visual texture and interest. There may be no walls separating the family room from the dining room, but a lowered ceiling or soffit over the dining table captures our eye and brings us into the space, making it feel more intimate. And don't just think about ceiling heights. A change in level of a step or two can invite us through an entry room to a slightly elevated family room and up again into a kitchen; a modest descending step can take us into a home office or master bedroom.

A soaring ceiling is not always what's wanted in a room—sometimes being a bit confined actually feels better. The dropped ceiling in this family room gives the space an intimate feel, while the dark color of the ceiling and the far walls helps to define the room's dimensions.

Family rooms like the one on the facing page are not the only spaces that can benefit from low ceilings. This dining area feels cozy at least in part because of its relatively low ceiling. Also helpful is the sense of enclosure created by walls and windows that hem it in handsomely on three sides.

A high, peaked ceiling makes a dramatic statement in this combination living and dining room. Amplifying the effect are the framed doorways on the far wall, which call attention to the ceiling height by stopping well short of it. Windows above each door ensure that light can travel freely between rooms.

light

Light dramatically alters our perception of space. Low windows, perhaps just inches above the floor, can pull the outdoors into a room, while narrow clerestory windows, properly positioned, not only permit privacy when space is an issue but also make a room feel bright and warm in winter and cool and shady in summer. Natural light spreading from a skylight in a small bedroom or long hallway opens up the space and gives you a visual sense of walls moving away from you rather than closing in (the philosophy behind all those small windows on airplanes).

Artificial lighting is equally important. Ambient lighting controlled by dimmers allows you to change the mood of even a small room from brightly cheerful to softly romantic. In a small bathroom with limited or no windows, the type and placement of lighting is particularly important. Several directional spots over a shower and vanity can seem to enlarge the entire room.

When considering fixtures versus lamps, factor in not just the aesthetics of the designs but the effect your choice will have on your small space. A floor lamp leaves a small bedside table uncluttered; sconces or ceiling spots eliminate the need for either.

What once was a solid wall at the end of the kitchen (left) is now open to light and views of the room on the other side. The cupboard fronts (below) are translucent; the back side facing the wall is clear glass, allowing lots of light into the kitchen.

Natural light makes its way into this small living room in two ways. There's the skylight, of course, but perhaps more important is the uninterrupted expanse of glass turning the corner of the wall behind the space-saving built-in couch.

Clerestory windows running just below the ceiling in the photo at left admit light into a bedroom with a lowered ceiling. Another way to get light into a confined space is via dormer windows, like the ones splashing light across the upstairs bedroom above.

architectural tricks

Architects use a number of techniques to increase the perception of spaciousness in a room. A curved soffit over a bathtub gives the illusion of a separate area without the need for a wall. Waist-high walls of glass blocks in a bathroom can have the same effect. Small cabinets, just large enough to hold brushes, combs, hair gel, or toothbrushes, can be almost invisible when built flush into the wall. This now-you-see-it-now-you-don't storage technique can also be used in kitchens, dining rooms, family rooms, and hallways to hide a wet bar, a media center, dinnerware, and sports gear.

Doors are another element where a little attention can bring large results. Pocket doors are perhaps the best-known space savers. Hidden in the wall between a kitchen and dining room, a pocket door can make both spaces feel larger. When closed, it hides meal preparation clutter while providing a warm, intimate space for dining. In a bathroom, a sandblasted glass entry door protects privacy while letting in ambient light from the bedroom.

And rather than solid walls between rooms, consider translucent panels along one wall of a living room, bedroom, or dining room. They can expand the perceived room size by giving visual intimations of adjacent spaces.

The pocket door to this bathroom takes up less space than a conventional swinging door—indeed, it's probably the only workable option, considering the narrowness of the corridor leading to the bedroom at the end of the hall, which has its own sliding door. To the right, a pocket window allows air circulation between rooms.

One popular architectural trick is to hide things in plain sight. The translucent cabinets in this dining area transform the dishes and glassware they store into colorful, hazy abstractions. The resulting grid is pleasing to the eye as well as supremely functional.

The trompe l'oeil treatment that wraps around this bed takes the edge off its hard surfaces. The illusion of soft bedding begins at the headboard, runs along the bed's base, and continues up the wall and onto the door leading to a bathroom. Note how the bathroom is partially open to the bedroom above the sink.

bonus spaces

When your space is limited, you have to not only maximize what's between the four walls of each room but also take advantage of odd nooks and crannies. Resourcefully transformed, bonus spaces like the area beneath stairs—usually either plastered over or left empty—can hold bookcases, a wine cellar, or stepped shelves. Drawers can even be designed into a staircase to hold rain gear, flashlights, household tools, or other occasionally used articles.

Crammed closets can be repurposed for entirely new uses. A linen closet near the kitchen can be turned into a walk-in pantry, one of the greatest luxuries for the small-space house. Not only does a pantry allow you to pack more things into a limited space than you could in the kitchen itself, it's also a natural organizer. A floor-to-ceiling shelving unit at the back of a pantry closet is typically no more than 4 feet long and a foot deep, yet its top shelf can hold a wok, a bread machine, or other infrequently used kitchen item, with room on the shelf below for enough canned goods to fill the equivalent of two kitchen cabinets. Staples like flour, sugar, and rice on another shelf still leave room for cooking oils, vinegars, baking ingredients, and, on the bottom level, as many as three dozen bottles of wine.

Bonus spaces sometimes take a bit of searching; other times they must be stolen outright. This area was only inches deep, but that was room enough for a mini-pantry to hold spices and canned goods.

A thick upholstered pad placed directly on the floor beneath a low, sloping ceiling converts wasted space into a relaxing spot for reading. An abundance of colorful pillows makes this bonus space even more attractive.

An alcove off a hallway (above) proved a convenient area to designate as an organizing center for papers and mail. Similarly, envisioning a corkboard on an underutilized section of wall (opposite) inspired a minor remodel; now shallow shelves, some slotted for mail, and a trio of drawers create a family message center.

A kid's desk fits in a corner along with bunk beds. The top bunk forms the roof of the compact study space, while the bottom bunk angles out to the side.

getting organized

We have *things*. And we need to put them *somewhere*. But where? There are two important principles for getting organized in a small space. The first is the rule of accessibility. That which we use regularly needs to be readily available; that which is seldom used can be hidden away. Holiday decorations and tax returns can be stored in plastic bins in an out-of-the-way place such as an attic. If you can carve a small closet out of your garage—say 4 feet by 5 feet—you can line it with inexpensive floor-to-ceiling shelving and fill it with plastic storage containers, putting the least-used items on the top.

The second rule of organization is to be creative. Old kitchen cabinets mounted high on garage walls are perfect for paper towels, toilet paper, picnic supplies, old publications, bottled water, and so on. The garage is also the perfect place for a small refrigerator—one just 30 inches high is big enough to chill more than two dozen bottles of wine. Reinforced garage rafters can hold surfboards, skis, rugs, and boxes. Outdoors, a shallow 3-foot-long cabinet above a garden bench safely stores gardening tools, seeds, bulbs, and fertilizers out of sight and out of the elements.

If you've got great stuff, don't hide it: put it on display! A collection of vintage plates and bowls, glass tumblers and pitchers, and ceramic containers of various sizes and shapes turns this kitchen into a mini-museum. Displaying by category (plates together, glasses together) heightens the overall impact.

The words "surprising" and "storage" don't usually go together, but these bicycles hung on a wall above a drafting table are a surprising storage solution if ever there was one. Bikes take up a lot a space, but they feel small here—and their shiny frames look stylish against the black wall.

Getting organized is all about the details. One simple storage solution is to build a drawer into a bench (above). Another quick fix is to install a steel rack inside a cabinet (right) so that pots and pans swivel into reach when the cabinet door is opened.

Part of this garage was remodeled with cabinets, open shelving, and overhead storage (accessible by a collapsible stair-ladder) to produce organization and efficiency in what was formerly a cluttered area with lots of wasted space.

jojo's notebook

small by design

"Efficiency begins at the advent of design." So says San Francisco-based architect and designer Richard Pennington.

Seems like a simple concept, right? But space efficiency isn't at the top of most homeowners' lists of wants and needs. Pennington believes we should pay attention to how our space is laid out and used. In fact, he's made space efficiency an art form, beginning with his own 850-square-foot home, where, he says, "We can entertain 40 people comfortably."

When it comes to his closets (right), Pennington favors a German system of modular components called ip20. "The height and depth of these cabinetry modules can be customized. The backs and fronts are finished, so the units are interchangeable and movable. And they're available in any exterior material you can imagine." By using these modular units, Pennington estimates he's achieved 85% storage efficiency versus the typical 62% of a traditional closet.

JoJo

The tall doors have a solid wood core that increases their durability

Wire racks on door interiors are low in profile and don't impede door operation

Modular units are movable—clothes closet today, kitchen pantry tomorrow!

Having a washer and dryer next to the closet makes laundry day a breeze

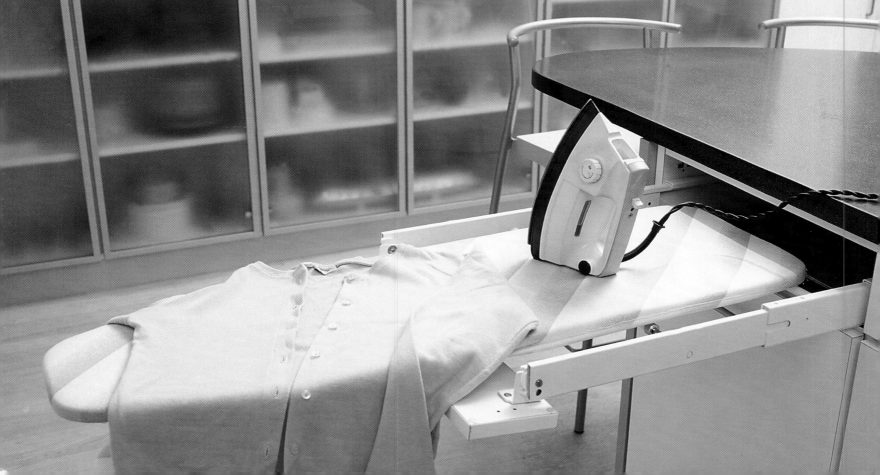

small wonders
space-saving stuff

window treatments ◉ desks ◉ tables ◉ dividers ◉ multi-function items
◉ fold-out beds ◉ hidden and half-size appliances ◉ prototypes

The Wow table comfortably seats six; its mocha-stained beech top unfolds from its aluminum frame. Available from The Conran Shop; conran.com.

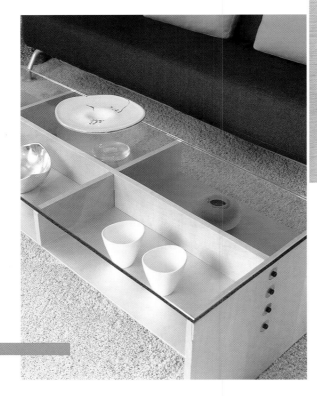

San Francisco designer Jeffrey Jones designed this coffee table, made of birch plywood and half-inch glass, to also function as a display case. Available by special order; JC2Jones@ sbcglobal.net.

The Kvadrant Triple Curtain Rail can be cut to size and mounts to ceilings or walls. This configuration features Anno Stra, Anno Horisont, and Anno Linje panels. Available from IKEA; ikea.com.

The Copenhagen Office Cabinet is a 3-foot-wide home office. Made of cherry or maple veneer, it has a file cabinet, drawer, pull-out desk top, and storage space. Available from Room & Board; roomandboard.com.

When opened, the circular cutouts on the Flipper folding screen become mini shelves that also let light pass between rooms. Available from Velocity; velocityartanddesign.com.

This multi-functional, wall-mounted workspace called the eNook is only 7.25 inches deep, but pull down its shelf and there's room for a laptop, iPod, cell phone, and digital camera. Available from Anthro; anthro.com.

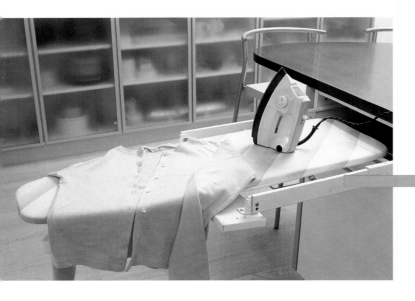

Combining two useful household items into one, the Ladder Kart is a stepladder that doubles as a hand truck and folds flat for easy storage. Available from Solutions; solutionscatalog.com.

Hiding an ironing board in a drawer is a great way to contain this typically bulky household item. Available from Modern Spaces: modernspaces.com.

You can run small, economical loads in the Drawer Dishwasher, and save shelf space by simply leaving clean dishes in one of the drawers until needed. Available from KitchenAid; kitchenaid.com.

The Houdini Wine Rack holds four bottles and folds flat when not in use. Units can be snapped together to create rows or stacks. Available from Metrokane; metrokane.com

The LGS single swivel bed (top) is similar to a traditional Murphy bed that folds out vertically from a wall. The Cabrio (right) folds out horizontally. The Cabrio doubles as a desk when not in use; the desk moves up and out of the way when the bed is opened. Available from Bonbon Trading; bonbon.co.uk.

Gas-assisted pistons make it easy to open and close The Computer Bed, which converts into a 29-inch-high workspace with room for a laptop and printer. Available from Flying Beds; flyingbeds.com.

future file | big things in small packages

When it comes to the space-saving ideas of tomorrow, innovative designers are pushing the envelope today. The birch plywood dining table and chairs on this page by Norwegian designers Alet and Dag Igland is called the Mealbox—it looks as if it were inspired by a Japanese bento lunch box. The six stools and table can be packed into a 27- by 30-inch box that's less than 18 inches high, yet the table, which fits together like a jigsaw puzzle, extends to 90 inches. For more information visit iglanddesign.orgdot.com.

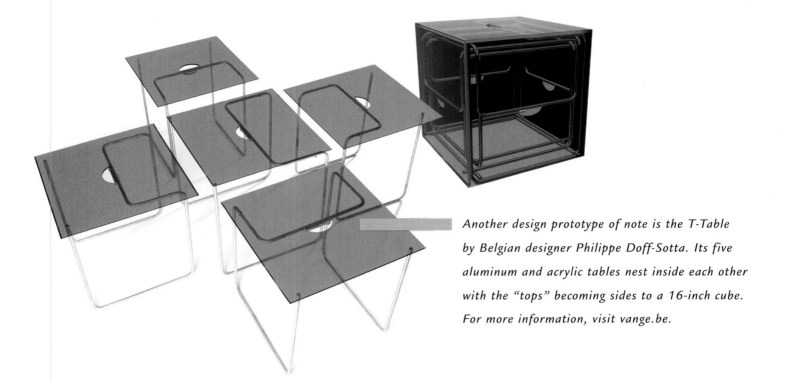

Another design prototype of note is the T-Table by Belgian designer Philippe Doff-Sotta. Its five aluminum and acrylic tables nest inside each other with the "tops" becoming sides to a 16-inch cube. For more information, visit vange.be.

For her final furniture studio project at the Pratt Institute in New York, industrial-design student Akemi Adrienne Tanaka created the Futaba coffee table out of bamboo plywood. The table, which takes its name from the Japanese word for two leaves sprouting from one seed, converts into a loveseat for "people with small apartments who like to entertain." For more information, visit akemitanaka.com.

jojo's notebook

tiny solutions

Tiny Living is getting big. The Manhattan store opened in 2005 with the mission of "helping New Yorkers furnish their famously tiny apartments." Since then word has spread and orders are rolling in from Tampa to Tokyo.

"We knew it was a good idea and that people would catch on to the concept. But we had no idea it'd catch on so fast," says co-owner Roee Dori, who created Tiny Living with his wife, Gretchen Broussard.

Roee and Gretchen sell products that are attractive, affordable, and absurdly efficient—whether it's collapsible Tupperware that squishes down to a storage-friendly one-inch thickness, or a 24-inch dining table that folds completely flat.

Currently Tiny Living's product line (see examples on the facing page) is displayed at their East Village store in Manhattan and is available online (tiny-living.com), but the couple hasn't ruled out opening more Tiny Living stores in selected markets.

JoJo

Tiny Living's teeny storefront in Manhattan

This Zem wine rack doubles as a bench. From chocolatefish.com.

The clear glass Ringo Side Table has a built-in magazine rack. From torretagus.com.

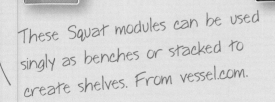

These Squat modules can be used singly as benches or stacked to create shelves. From vessel.com.

The circular Moon table folds flat. From gotoeurostyle.com.

design credits

front matter
1 *Architect:* EDI Architecture; *Interior Design:* Pamela Pennington Studios, pamelapenningtonstudios.com; *Chairs and mirror:* Crate & Barrel, crateandbarrel.com 2 left Michael Blatt, Fung + Blatt Architects, fungandblatt.com 3 center Malcolm Davis Architecture, malcolmdavisaia.com 3 bottom right *Design:* Richard Pennington/ Modern Spaces, modernspaces.com

small inspirations
7 *Garden design:* Judy McGowan

big ideas | room by room
10 bottom *Architect:* Patrick Tighe 11 HhLodesign, hhlodesign.com 12 Place Architecture, placearch.com 13 Bates + Masi Architects, batesmasi.com 15 bottom right Ronald W. Madson, Madson Associates 19 Pamela Pennington Studios, pamelapenningtonstudios.com 20–21 Laurie Ghielmetti and Douglas McDonald, Laurie Ghielmetti Interiors, lghielmetti@sigprop.com 21 *Kitchen Design:* Bulthaup 22 top Levy Art & Architecture; Drew Maran Construction/ Design, drewmaran.com; Sandra Slater Environments, sandraslater.com 22 bottom Gordon Olschlager 23 top left Byron Kuth and Elizabeth Ranieri, Kuth/Ranieri Architects, kuthranieri.com 23 bottom left Lorri Kershner/L. Kershner Design, lkershnerdesign.com 25 bottom Michelle Kaufmann Designs, mkd-arc.com 26 bottom Lisa Joyce/Lisa Joyce Architecture, lisajoyce@sbcglobal.net; Peter Kyle/Woodworks Construction & Design, pkyle@sbcglobal.net 27 left and top right *Styling:* Emma Star Jensen 28–29 all *Architect:* Jerome Buttrick 30–31 all *Design:* Charlotte & Jeffrey Jones 32 *Architect:* EDI Architecture; *Interior Design:* Pamela Pennington Studios, pamelapenningtonstudios.com 34 all *Design:* P Kirkeby, Inc., pkirkeby.com 36 top right *Original architect:* Richard Neutra; *Restoration architect:* Chad Overway 36 bottom right Kent and Pam Greene 37 HhLodesign, hhlodesign.com 38 all *Kitchen:* David Huisman/Chalon US, chalonus.com; *Interior:* Mauvianne Giusti/Bella Villa Designs 39 top right Lisa Joyce/Lisa Joyce Architecture, lisajoyce@sbcglobal.net; Peter Kyle/Woodworks Construction & Design, pkyle@sbcglobal.net 39 bottom left *Design:* Jennifer Hodges 40 all Dan & Lonny Danenberg/Kitchens By Design, danenbergdesigns.com 41 top *Design:* Richard Pennington/ Modern Spaces, modernspaces.com 42–43 all Bates + Masi Architects, batesmasi.com 44–45 top and 45 top right and right Malcolm Davis Architecture, malcolmdavisaia.com 46 top right Stephen Dynia Architects, dynia.com 47 bottom left Clark Interiors 47 top right *Design:* Nina Bookbinder 48 top Malcolm Davis Architecture, malcolmdavisaia.com 48 bottom left and right *Interior Design:* Lydia Corser/EcoInteriors; *General Contractor:* Brian Corser/Corser Home Services 49 top left Jim Smith, Agency for Architecture 49 right *Design:* Gregory Ciurczak 49 bottom left Crespi Woodworking 50 top right William Rawn Associates, Architects, rawnarch.com 50 bottom left David Coleman/Architecture, davidcoleman.com 50 bottom right *Design:* Laurie Ghielmetti and Douglas McDonald, Laurie Ghielmetti Interiors, lghielmetti@sigprop.com;

Kitchen Design: Bulthaup 51 left Malcolm Davis Architecture, malcolm-davisaia.com 52–53 all *Architect:* Peter Pfau 54–56 all Malcolm Davis Architecture, malcolmdavisaia.com 58 top Jarvis Architects 58 bottom Patricia McDonald and Marcia Moore 59 top right Gregory T. Carmichael Interior Design and Geoffrey Prentiss, Prentiss Architect 60 top left Harlan Pedersen, Architect, AIA 60 top right *Architect:* Dennis Diego, AIA 61 *Architect:* EDI Architecture; *Interior Design:* Pamela Pennington Studios, pamelapenningtonstudios.com; *Chairs and mirror:* Crate & Barrel, crate-andbarrel.com 63 top left Byron Kuth and Elizabeth Ranieri, Kuth/Ranieri Architects, kuthranieri.com 63 bottom right Roger P. Kurath, Design 21, and Vance Lorenzini, Lorenzini Design 64–65 all *Design:* Lorri Kershner/ L. Kershner Design, lkershnerdesign.com 67 *Design:* Stephanie Heit 69 Cary Bernstein Architect, cbstudio.com 71 bottom right *Design:* Gregory Ciurczak 72 top left Michael Blatt, Fung + Blatt Architects, fungandblatt.com 73 right and bottom Paul Scardina 74 top right Swerve C. of California and Goldin Design 75 bottom left Sasha Emerson Design Studio 76–77 all Malcolm Davis Architecture, malcolmdavisaia.com 78 all *Architect:* COOP 15, coop15.com; *Design:* Amy Baker Interior Design, amybakerdesign.com 79 top left *Architect:* Patrick Tighe 82 bottom left Crespi Woodworking 82 top right Jennifer Cheh Design Studio 83 bottom left David Wright Associates 83 top right Joshua Coggeshall Cog Work Shop 84–85 all *Cabinetry:* P Kirkeby, Inc., pkirkeby.com 89 Alejandro Ortiz Architects 91 top left Veverka Architects 92 top left Arkin-Tilt Architects 92 bottom right Ron Sutton, Sutton Suzuki Architects, suttonsuzukiarchitects.com 92 bottom left *Architect:* Jerome Buttrick 94 bottom left Michael Mullin Architect, michaelmullin.com 94 top right SkB Architects 95 bottom left Sant Architects 97 top left Patricia Brennan Architects, patriciabrennanarchitects.com 97 bottom right Marmol Radziner + Associates, marmol-radziner.com 98–99 all Byron Kuth and Elizabeth Ranieri, Kuth/Ranieri Architects, kuthranieri.com 100–101 all *Design:* JoAnn Masaoka Van Atta; *Tile:* Phillip Knowles/ Ceramic & Stone Design; *Cabinetry Finish:* Pigments of Imagination/Karen Talbott 102 Veverka Architects 103 Jennifer Cheh Design Studio 105 top left Kathleen Navarra, Navarra Design, Inc., navarradesign.com 105 bottom right Satterberg Desonier Dumo Interior Design, satterberg design.com 106 top left Lisa Malloy/ Interior Inspirations 106 top right Carey DiPrima 106 bottom right David Stark Wilson/Wilson Architects 107 Mark A. Hutker/Mark Hutker Associates & Architects Inc. 110 top left Linda Brettler Architect 110–111 top Joann Le and David Horsley, DAO Architecture 110 bottom right Patkau Architects, patkau.ca 111 right and bottom Mike Mora, Heliotrope Architects, heliotrope.cc; Amy Baker Interior Design, amybakerdesign.com 112–113 all *Architect:* Lorcan O'Herlihy 114–115 all *Design:* Sandra C. Watkins 116 Mark Wienke, markwienke.com 118 top left David Wright Associates 118 top right Alejandro Ortiz Architects, ortizarchitects.com 119 top *Architect:* Patrick Tighe 120–121 all Michelle Kaufmann Designs, mkd-arc.com

big concepts | maxing your space
122 top Arkin-Tilt Architects 123 Byron Kuth and Elizabeth Ranieri, Kuth/Ranieri Architects, kuthranieri.com 124 *Design:* Richard Pennington/Modern Spaces, modernspaces.com 125 bottom right Nick Noyes Architecture, nnarchitecture.

com **126 top right** Lindy Small Architecture **126 bottom left** *Cabinetry:* P Kirkeby, Inc., pkirkeby.com **127 top right** Cary Bernstein Architect, cbstudio.com **127 bottom left** *Architect:* Lee Phillips; *Builder:* Geoff Welch **128** Levy Art & Architecture; Drew Maran Construction/ Design, drewmaran.com; Sandra Slater Environments, sandraslater.com **129** Kent Means, AIA, MacArthur, Means & Wells architecture, mmwarchitects.com **130 top left** Pamela Pennington Studios, pamelapenningtonstudios.com **130 bottom right** *Architect:* Jerry Waters **131 top left** Kent and Pam Greene **132** Bethe Cohen **133 top left** Dennis Deppmeier, AIA, A&E Architects, aearchitects.com **133 bottom right** *Design:* L. Kershner Design, lkershnerdesign.com; *Architect:* Tom Thacher/Thacher & Thompson Architects; *Handblown Vessels:* Kanik Chung **134 top left** Place Architecture, placearch.com **134 bottom right** Tish Key Interior Design **135 top left** *Architect:* Patrick Tighe **135 bottom left** Schwartz and Architecture, schwartzandarchitecture.com **136** Sant Architects **137 all** Byron Kuth and Elizabeth Ranieri, Kuth/Ranieri Architects, kuthranieri.com **138 center** Malcolm Davis Architecture, malcolmdavisaia.com **138 bottom right** Andre Rothblatt Architecture **139 top left** *Architect:* Bruce Teel **140** Sacha Emerson Design Studio **141 top left** Gregory T. Carmichael Interior Design and Geoffrey Prentiss, Prentiss Architects **141 center** *Interior Design:* Lydia Corser/EcoInteriors; *General Contractor:* Brian Corser/Corser Home Services **141 right and 143** *Design:* Richard Pennington/Modern Spaces, modernspaces.com

small wonders|space-saving stuff **144 top** *Design:* Charlotte & Jeffrey Jones **144 bottom** *Design:* Richard Pennington/ Modern Spaces, modernspaces.com **146 center right** *Design:* Charlotte & Jeffrey Jones **146 bottom left** *Design:* Jeffrey Jones **148 top left** *Design:* Richard Pennington/Modern Spaces, modernspaces.com

photography credits

courtesy **Akemi Adrienne Tanaka:** 151 bottom left and bottom right; courtesy **Anthro Corporation:** 145, 147 right; courtesy **Bates + Masi Architects:** 13, 42–43 all; beateworks.com: 135 right; **Laurie Black:** 73 top right and bottom; courtesy **Bonbon Trading:** 149 top; **Marion Brenner:** 36 bottom left, 122 bottom; **Gay Bumgarner/Positive Images:** 119 bottom right; **Ed Caldwell:** 92 top left; **Benny Chan:** 97 bottom right; **Ken Chen:** 33 top right, 96 top left, 141 bottom left; courtesy **Chocolate Fish:** 153 top right; courtesy **The Conran Shop:** 146 top left and center; **Grey Crawford:** 63 bottom right, 105 top left; **Malcolm Davis:** 45 top right and bottom right; **Joseph De Leo:** 45 bottom left, 59 bottom left, 93 all; © **Disney Enterprises, Inc.:** 4–5 all; **Phillip Ennis:** 41 bottom, 44 top left, 62 top right, 73 top left, 109 all, 131 bottom right; courtesy **Euro Style:** 153 bottom center; **Andrew Faulkner Photography:** 51 top left, 54–55 all, 76–77 all; **Diane Faulkner:** 44–45 top; courtesy **FlyingBeds:** 149 center and bottom right; **William Geddes/beateworks.com:** 139 bottom; **Tria Giovan:** 14, 15 top left, 35 top left, 46 top left and bottom left, 60 bottom right, 75 right and top left, 96 bottom right, 117, 118 bottom right; **John Granen:** 49 top left, 50 bottom left, 94 top right, 106 top right; **Art Gray:** 10 bottom, 50 top right, 79 top left, 110 top left, 116, 118 top right, 119 top left, 135 top left; **Ken Gutmaker:** 138 bottom right; **Jamie Hadley:** 3 bottom right, 20–21 all, 23 bottom left, 26 bottom right, 27 bottom right, 30–31 all, 34 all, 38–40 all, 41 top, 47 top right, 48 bottom left and bottom right, 49 right, 50 bottom right, 57, 58 top right, 60 top right, 64–65 all, 67, 71 bottom right, 74 top right, 75 bottom left, 84–85 all, 91 top left, 98–102 all, 106 top left, 106 bottom right, 107, 108 top left, 114–115 all, 123, 124, 126 bottom left, 127 bottom left, 133 bottom right, 137 bottom left, 140, 141 center and right, 143, 144 all, 146 right and bottom left, 148 top left; **Margot Hartford:** 15 bottom right, 47 bottom left; **Alex Hayden:** 11, 36 bottom right, 37, 59 top right, 78 all, 105 bottom right, 111 right and bottom right, 131 top left, 141 top left; courtesy **Igland Design:** 150 all; **Michael Jensen:** 97 top left; **Muffy Kibbey:** 58 bottom left, 132; courtesy **KitchenAid:** 148 bottom center; **Dennis Krukowski:** 62 left, 108 bottom right; **J. K. Lawrence:** 12, 46 top right, 60 top left, 129, 133 top left, 134 top left; **Catherine Ledner:** 24 top left, 104 top left; **davidduncanlivingston.com:** 80 top right; courtesy **Metrokane:** 148 bottom left; **Wendy Nordeck:** 22 top right, 128 bottom; **David Papazian:** 130 bottom right; **Norm Plate:** 7; **Marvin Rand:** 22 bottom left; **Lisa Romerein:** 2 left, 72 top left, 82 top right, 83 top right, 89, 95 bottom left, 103, 110–111 top, 125 bottom right, 136; courtesy **Room and Board:** 147 top left; **Cesar Rubio:** 52–53 all; **Jeremy Samuelson:** 10 top, 68, 70 left, 72 bottom left, 74 bottom left, 79 bottom right, 80 bottom left, 81 top right, 87–88 all, 91 bottom right, 95 top right, 125 top; **Christina Schmidhofer:** 49 bottom left, 82 bottom left; **Michael Skott:** 16–17 all; courtesy **Solutions:** 148 top center and top right; **Thomas J. Story:** cover, 1, 23 top left, 24 bottom right, 25 bottom right, 27 left and top right, 28–29 all, 32, 36 top right, 61 right, 63 top left, 69, 90 all, 92 bottom right and bottom left, 94 bottom left, 110 bottom right, 118 top left, 120–121 all, 122 top, 126 top right, 127 top right, 134 bottom right, 134 bottom left, 137 top right, 139 top left; **Tim Street-Porter:** 2–3 top, 6, 8–9 all, 35 bottom right, 51 bottom right, 70–71 top, 81 bottom left, 104 bottom right, 139 top right; courtesy **Tiny Living:** 152 left; courtesy **Torre & Tagus:** 3 bottom left, 153 bottom right; courtesy **Travis Industries:** 26 top left; courtesy **Vange:** 151 top left and top right; courtesy **Velocity Art and Design:** 147 center and bottom left; **Michal Venera:** 3 center, 48 top, 56, 138 center; courtesy **Vessel:** 153 left; **David Wakely:** 51 top right; **Michael Weschler:** 112–113 all; **Peter O. Whiteley:** 83 bottom left; **Eric Zepeda:** 19, 130 top left

acknowledgments *We would like to extend special thanks to Richard Pennington at Modern Spaces (modernspaces.com), Quinn Morgan and Malcolm Davis at Malcolm Davis Architecture (malcolmdavisaia.com), Paul Masi at Bates + Masi Architects (batesmasi.com), and Roee Dori and Gretchen Broussard at Tiny Living (tiny-living.com). Thanks also to Thomas J. Story, E. Spencer Toy, and Sara Luce Jamison at Sunset magazine.*

index